# CASSEROLES & STEWS

Consultant Editor:
Valerie Ferguson

LORENZ BOOKS

# Contents

# Introduction

Casseroles and stews involve cooking meat, poultry, game or fish slowly in liquid along with vegetables and flavourings. In this fast-food era, they are often overlooked, but in fact they have many advantages. Certainly meat, poultry and game versions are usually cooked for a relatively long time, but for this reason they can transform cheaper cuts into delicious and economical meals. Because the food is cooked in liquid, a sauce is produced that is bursting with flavour and which locks in the nutrients of the main ingredients.

Casseroles and stews are extremely convenient for busy people as they can be left while the cook gets on with other things. They may be prepared in advance and reheated: the flavour actually develops while they are "resting", perhaps overnight in the fridge. They also freeze well.

There is a huge range of recipes for every occasion, from all parts of the world. Irish Stew or Harvest Vegetable & Lentil Casserole would make an ideal family supper. For a dinner party, Pheasant with Juniper & Port or Creole Fish Stew would win compliments. Try them and enjoy the special pleasure to be had in eating a good casserole or stew.

# Stock

Good-quality stock is essential for casseroles and stews and it is worth the effort to prepare it at home. Home-made stock may be frozen successfully for several months.

## Fish Stock

INGREDIENTS
1 onion
1 carrot
1 celery stick
any fish bones, skin and
    trimmings available
6 black peppercorns
2 bay leaves
3 fresh parsley sprigs

**1** Peel and coarsely slice the onion. Peel and chop the carrot, and scrub and slice the celery.

**2** Place the prepared vegetables with all the other ingredients in a large saucepan and add enough water to cover. Bring the water to the boil, skim the surface and simmer, uncovered, for 20 minutes. The stock can either be strained and used immediately or stored for up to two days in the fridge and used as required.

## Brown Stock

INGREDIENTS
30 ml/2 tbsp vegetable oil
675 g/1½ lb shin of beef untrimmed,
    cut into pieces
1 bouquet garni
2 onions, trimmed and quartered
2 carrots, trimmed and chopped
2 celery sticks, sliced
5 ml/1 tsp black peppercorns
2.5 ml/½ tsp salt

**1** Preheat the oven to 220°C/425°F/ Gas 7. Drizzle the vegetable oil over the bottom of a roasting tin and then add the meat. Coat in the oil and bake for 25–30 minutes, or until well browned, turning regularly to ensure even browning.

**2** Transfer the meat to a large saucepan, add the remaining ingredients and cover with 3.2 litres/ 5½ pints/14 cups water. Bring to the boil, skim the surface, then partially cover and simmer for 2½–3 hours, or until reduced to 1.75 litres/3 pints/ 7½ cups.

**3** Strain the stock and allow to cool; remove the solidified fat before use. Store for up to four days in the fridge.

# Chicken or White Stock

INGREDIENTS
1 onion
4 cloves
1 carrot
2 leeks
2 celery sticks
1 cooked or raw chicken carcass or
    675 g/1½ lb veal bones,
    cut into pieces
1 bouquet garni
8 black peppercorns
2.5 ml/½ tsp salt

**1** Peel the onion, cut into quarters and spike each quarter with a clove. Scrub and roughly chop the remaining vegetables. Place the vegetables in a large saucepan with the rest of the ingredients for the stock.

**2** Cover with 1.75 litres/3 pints/ 7½ cups water. Bring to the boil, skim the surface and simmer, partially covered, for 2 hours. Strain and allow to cool. When cold, remove the hardened fat before using. Store for up to four days in the fridge.

# Vegetable Stock

INGREDIENTS
1 onion
2 carrots
2 large celery sticks
small amounts of any of the following:
    leeks, celeriac, parsnip, turnip,
    cabbage or cauliflower trimmings,
    mushroom peelings
30 ml/2 tbsp vegetable oil
1 bouquet garni
6 black peppercorns

**1** Peel and slice the onion. Scrub and roughly chop the carrots, celery and remaining vegetables.

**2** Heat the oil in a large pan and fry all the vegetables until soft and lightly browned. Add the remaining ingredients and cover with 1.75 litres/ 3 pints/7½ cups water.

**3** Bring the water to the boil, skim the surface, then partially cover and simmer for 1½ hours. Strain the stock and allow to cool. Store the stock in the fridge for up to three days.

# Mediterranean Fish Stew

Probably the most famous fish stew, *bouillabaisse* is found in many variations.

Serves 8

INGREDIENTS

2.75 kg/6 lb white fish, such as sea bass,
    snapper or monkfish (choose thick fish),
    filleted, skinned and cut into even pieces
45 ml/3 tbsp extra virgin olive oil
grated rind of 1 orange
1 garlic clove, very finely chopped
pinch of saffron threads
30 ml/2 tbsp pastis (anise liqueur)
1 small fennel bulb, finely chopped
1 large onion, finely chopped
225 g/8 oz small new potatoes, sliced
900 g/2 lb large raw prawns, peeled
salt and freshly ground black pepper
croûtons, to serve

FOR THE STOCK

2 leeks, sliced
1 onion, halved and sliced
1 red pepper, cored and sliced
30 ml/2 tbsp olive oil
1–1.5 kg/2¼–3 lb fish heads, bones
675 g/1½ lb ripe tomatoes, quartered
4 garlic cloves, sliced
1 bouquet garni
thinly pared rind of ½ orange
2 or 3 pinches saffron threads

FOR THE *ROUILLE*

25 g/1 oz/½ cup soft white breadcrumbs
1 or 2 garlic cloves, very finely chopped
½ red pepper, roasted
5 ml/1 tsp tomato purée
120 ml/4 fl oz/½ cup extra virgin olive oil

**1** Put the fish in a bowl with 30 ml/ 2 tbsp of the oil, the orange rind, garlic, saffron and pastis. Turn to coat well, cover and chill.

**2** To make the stock, cook the leeks, onion and pepper in a pan for about 5 minutes. Add the remaining ingredients and enough water to cover. Bring to the boil, skim, then simmer, covered, for 30 minutes. Strain.

**3** To make the *rouille,* soak the breadcrumbs in water, then squeeze dry. Process in a food processor with the garlic, roasted red pepper and tomato purée until smooth. With the machine running, slowly pour in the oil.

**4** To finish the stew, cook the fennel and onion for about 5 minutes in the remaining olive oil, then add the prepared stock. Bring the mixture to the boil, add the sliced new potatoes and cook for 5–7 minutes.

**5** Reduce the heat and add the fish, starting with the thickest pieces, then the prawns. Simmer until all the fish and shellfish are cooked. Season to taste and serve with croûtons spread with the *rouille*.

# Creole Fish Stew

A simple, attractive dish – good for a dinner party.

Serves 4–6

INGREDIENTS
2 red bream or large snapper, prepared
    and cut into 2.5 cm/1 in pieces
30 ml/2 tbsp malt vinegar
flour, for dusting
oil, for frying

FOR THE SAUCE
30 ml/2 tbsp oil
15 ml/1 tbsp butter or margarine
1 onion, finely chopped
275 g/10 oz tomatoes, peeled and
    finely chopped
2 garlic cloves, crushed
2 fresh thyme sprigs
600 ml/1 pint/2½ cups fish stock or water
2.5 ml/½ tsp ground cinnamon
1 hot chilli, seeded and chopped
115 g/4 oz each red and green pepper,
    finely chopped
salt
fresh oregano sprigs, to garnish

FOR THE SPICE SEASONING
15 ml/1 tbsp garlic granules
7.5 ml/1½ tsp freshly ground
    black pepper
7.5 ml/1½ tsp paprika
7.5 ml/1½ tsp celery salt
7.5 ml/1½ tsp curry powder
5 ml/1 tsp caster sugar

**1** To make the spice seasoning, mix all the ingredients together.

**2** Sprinkle the fish with 30 ml/2 tbsp spice seasoning and vinegar, turning to coat. Set aside to marinate for at least 2 hours or overnight in the fridge.

**3** When you are ready to cook the fish, place a little flour on a large plate and coat the fish pieces all over, shaking off any excess.

**4** Heat a little oil in a pan and fry the fish for about 5 minutes until it is golden brown, then set it aside. Don't worry if the fish is not cooked through it will finish cooking in the sauce.

**5** To make the sauce, heat the oil and butter or margarine in a large frying pan or wok and stir-fry the onion for 5 minutes. Add the tomatoes, garlic and thyme, stir well and simmer for a further 5 minutes. Stir in the stock or water, cinnamon and chilli.

**6** Add the fish pieces and the chopped peppers to the stock mixture. Simmer until the fish is cooked through and the stock has reduced to a thick sauce. Season with salt to taste. Serve the stew hot, garnished with fresh oregano sprigs.

# Fish Stew with Lemon Grass

Lemon grass gives this delicate fish casserole an aromatic flavour, perfect for a special treat.

Serves 4

INGREDIENTS

25 g/1 oz/2 tbsp butter
175 g/6 oz onions, chopped
20 ml/4 tsp plain flour
400 ml/14 fl oz/1⅔ cups stock
150 ml/¼ pint/⅔ cup white wine
2.5 cm/1 in piece fresh root ginger, peeled
    and finely chopped
2 lemon grass stalks, trimmed and
    finely chopped
450 g/1 lb new potatoes, scrubbed and
    halved if necessary
450 g/1 lb white fish fillets, skinned
175 g/6 oz large peeled cooked prawns
275 g/10 oz small broccoli florets
150 ml/¼ pint/⅔ cup double cream
60 ml/4 tbsp chopped fresh garlic chives
salt and freshly ground black pepper
crusty bread, to serve

**2** Stir in the stock, white wine, ginger, lemon grass and potatoes. Season well with salt and freshly ground black pepper and bring to the boil. Cover and cook for 15 minutes or until the potatoes are almost tender.

**3** Cut the fish fillets into large chunks. Add these to the pan with the cooked prawns, broccoli florets and double cream. Stir gently.

**4** Simmer gently for 5 minutes, taking care not to break up the fish. Adjust the seasoning and stir in the garlic chives. Serve the stew with plenty of crusty bread.

**1** Melt the butter in a large saucepan. Cook the onions for 3–4 minutes or until just tender. Stir in the flour and cook for 1 minute.

# French Fish Stew

A traditional recipe using freshwater fish and brandy.

Serves 6

INGREDIENTS
1.5 kg/3–3½ lb freshwater fish, such as carp,
   trout and skinned eel
45 ml/3 tbsp plain flour
50 g/2 oz/4 tbsp butter
225 g/8 oz smoked bacon, cut into thin strips
4 shallots, very finely chopped
225 g/8 oz small onions
225 g/8 oz/3 cups mushrooms, chopped
120 ml/4 fl oz/½ cup brandy
1 litre/1¾ pints/4 cups red wine
300 ml/½ pint/1¼ cups veal or chicken stock
1 garlic clove, crushed
1 bouquet garni
salt and freshly ground black pepper
chopped fresh parsley, to garnish
garlic bread, to serve

**1** Clean the carp and trout, remove the heads and fins, fillet the flesh and cut into slices. Cut the eel into chunks. Put half the flour into a plastic bag, season, add all the fish pieces and shake to coat.

**2** In a large pan, melt the butter and brown the fish pieces on both sides. Remove from the pan and set aside.

**3** Add the bacon, shallots and onions to the pan and cook over a low heat for a further 10 minutes until golden. Stir in the mushrooms and cook for a further 5 minutes.

**4** Pour in the brandy, stir and flambé (optional). Add the red wine and simmer for a few minutes.

**5** Stir in the stock, garlic and bouquet garni, bring to the boil and simmer for 5 minutes. Add the fish and simmer until cooked.

**6** With a slotted spoon, remove the fish and keep hot. In a small bowl, blend the remaining flour with a little cold water and stir into the pan. Bring to the boil and cook for 5 minutes, then return the fish to the pan. Serve garnished with chopped parsley and accompanied by garlic bread.

# Fish Stew with Calvados, Parsley & Dill

This rustic stew combines all sorts of interesting flavours and will please and intrigue anyone who tastes it. Many varieties of fish can be used: just choose the freshest and the best that is available.

Serves 4

INGREDIENTS
1 kg/2¼ lb assorted white fish
15 ml/1 tbsp chopped fresh flat leaf parsley,
   plus a few leaves to garnish
225 g/8 oz/3 cups small mushrooms
225 g/8 oz can tomatoes
10 ml/2 tsp flour
15 g/½ oz/1 tbsp butter
450 ml/¾ pint/scant
   2 cups cider
45 ml/3 tbsp Calvados
1 large bunch fresh dill, plus a few fronds,
   to garnish
salt and freshly ground
   black pepper

**1** Preheat the oven to 180°C/350°F/ Gas 4. Roughly chop the fish and place it in a casserole with the parsley, mushrooms, tomatoes and salt and pepper to taste.

**2** Work the flour into the butter. Heat the cider and stir in the flour and butter mixture a little at a time. Cook, stirring, until it has thickened slightly.

**3** Add the cider mixture and the remaining ingredients to the fish, reserving a few dill fronds for the garnish. Mix gently, cover and bake for about 30 minutes. Serve garnished with dill fronds and parsley leaves.

# Seafarer's Stew

Smoked haddock gives this stew its distinctive flavour.

Serves 4

### INGREDIENTS
225 g/8 oz undyed smoked
  haddock fillet
225 g/8 oz fresh monkfish fillet
20 fresh mussels, scrubbed
1 shallot, finely chopped
2 streaky bacon rashers (optional),
  cut into strips
15 ml/1 tbsp olive oil
225 g/8 oz carrots,
  coarsely grated
150 ml/¼ pint/⅔ cup single or
  double cream
115 g/4 oz cooked peeled prawns
salt and freshly ground
  black pepper
30 ml/2 tbsp chopped fresh parsley,
  to garnish

**1** In a large pan, simmer the fish in 1.2 litres/2 pints/5 cups water for 5 minutes. Add the mussels, cover and cook for 5 minutes more or until all the mussels have opened. Discard any that have not.

**2** Drain, reserving the liquid. Return the liquid to the pan. Flake the haddock and cut the monkfish into large chunks.

**3** Fry the shallot and bacon in the oil for 3–4 minutes. Add to the strained fish broth, bring to the boil, then add the carrots and cook for 10 minutes.

**4** Stir in the cream, fish, mussels and prawns. Heat gently, without boiling. Season and garnish with parsley.

# Fricassée of Chicken

A fricassée is a classic dish in which poultry or meat is first seared in fat, then braised with liquid until cooked.

Serves 4–6

INGREDIENTS
50 g/2 oz/4 tbsp butter
30 ml/2 tbsp oil
1.2–1.5 kg/2½–3 lb chicken,
　cut into pieces
25 g/1 oz/¼ cup plain flour
250 ml/8 fl oz/1 cup dry
　white wine
750 ml/1¼ pints/3 cups
　chicken stock
1 bouquet garni
1.5 ml/¼ tsp white pepper
225 g/8 oz/3 cups button
　mushrooms, trimmed
5 ml/1 tsp lemon juice
16–24 small white
　onions, peeled
120 ml/4 fl oz/½ cup water
5 ml/1 tsp sugar
90 ml/6 tbsp whipping cream
salt
30 ml/2 tbsp chopped fresh parsley,
　to garnish

**3** Add the wine, stock, bouquet garni, salt and white pepper. Bring to the boil, cover and simmer for 25–30 minutes until the chicken is tender and cooked through. Transfer the chicken to a serving dish and keep warm. Discard the bouquet garni.

**1** Melt half the butter with the oil in a flameproof casserole and fry the chicken in batches for 10 minutes or until just golden.

**2** Sprinkle in the flour, turning the chicken pieces to ensure they are evenly coated. Cook gently for about 4 minutes.

**4** Meanwhile, in a frying pan, heat the remaining butter and cook the mushrooms and lemon juice for 3–4 minutes. Transfer to a bowl.

**5** Add the onions, water and sugar to the pan and simmer for 10 minutes, until just tender. Strain the onions and add them to the mushrooms. Set aside.

**6** Add any vegetable juices to the stock in the casserole. Boil until reduced by half. Whisk in the cream and cook for 2 minutes.

**7** Add the vegetables and cook for 2 minutes more. Adjust the seasoning, pour the sauce over the chicken, garnish with parsley and serve.

# Pot-roast Chicken with Lemon & Garlic

This rustic dish is easy to prepare. Lardons are thick strips of bacon fat; if you can't get them, use streaky bacon.

Serves 4

INGREDIENTS

30 ml/2 tbsp olive oil
25 g/1 oz/2 tbsp butter
175 g/6 oz/1 cup smoked lardons or
    roughly chopped streaky bacon
8 garlic cloves, peeled
4 onions, quartered
10 ml/2 tsp plain flour
600 ml/1 pint/2½ cups chicken stock
2 lemons, thickly sliced
45 ml/3 tbsp chopped fresh thyme
1.5 kg/3–3½ lb chicken
2 x 400 g/14 oz cans flageolet beans,
    drained and rinsed
salt and freshly ground black pepper
bread, to serve

**1** Preheat the oven to 190°C/375°F/ Gas 5. Heat the oil and butter in a flameproof casserole that is large enough to hold the chicken with a little extra room around the sides. Add the lardons or bacon and cook until golden. Remove with a slotted spoon and drain on kitchen paper.

**2** Brown the garlic and onions over a medium heat until the edges are caramelized. Stir in the flour, then the stock. Return the bacon to the pan with the lemons, thyme and seasoning.

**3** Bring to the boil, then place the chicken on top and season. Cover and cook in the oven for 1 hour, basting the chicken occasionally.

**4** Baste the chicken with the juices. Stir the beans into the casserole and return it to the oven for a further 30 minutes or until the chicken is cooked through and tender.

**5** Carve the chicken into thick slices and serve with the beans and plenty of bread, to mop up the juices.

# Chicken, Leek & Bacon Casserole

A moist whole chicken, braised on a bed of leeks and bacon and topped with a creamy tarragon sauce.

Serves 4–6

INGREDIENTS
15 ml/1 tbsp oil
25 g/1 oz/2 tbsp butter
1.5 kg/3–3½ lb chicken
225 g/8 oz streaky bacon
450 g/1 lb leeks
250 ml/8 fl oz/1 cup chicken stock
250 ml/8 fl oz/1 cup double cream
15 ml/1 tbsp chopped
    fresh tarragon
salt and freshly ground
    black pepper

**1** Preheat the oven to 180°C/350°F/ Gas 4. Heat the oil and butter in a large flameproof casserole.

**2** Add the chicken to the casserole and cook it, breast side up, for 5 minutes until it is golden brown. Remove from the casserole.

**3** Dice the bacon and add to the casserole. Cook for 4–5 minutes until golden. Cut the leeks into 2.5 cm/1 in pieces and add to the bacon. Cook, stirring occasionally, for 5 minutes until the leeks begin to brown.

**4** Put the chicken on top of the bacon and leeks. Cover and cook in the oven for 1½ hours.

**5** Remove the chicken, bacon and leeks from the casserole. Skim the fat from the juices left in the casserole. Pour in the chicken stock and double cream and bring the mixture to the boil. Cook for 4–5 minutes until the sauce is slightly reduced and thickened.

**6** Stir in the tarragon and seasoning (only pepper may be needed). Serve the chicken in slices with the bacon, leeks and a little sauce.

# Coq au Vin

Chicken is casseroled with red wine to make this fine classic dish.

Serves 4

INGREDIENTS
15 ml/1 tbsp olive oil
50 g/2 oz/4 tbsp butter
20 baby onions
75 g/3 oz piece streaky bacon
    without rind, diced
about 20 button mushrooms
1.5 kg/3–3½ lb chicken,
    cut into 8 joints
45 ml/3 tbsp plain flour
30 ml/2 tbsp brandy
75 cl bottle red Burgundy wine
1 bouquet garni
3 garlic cloves
5 ml/1 tsp soft light brown sugar
*beurre manié* made with 15 ml/1 tbsp each
    of butter and plain flour
salt and freshly ground
    black pepper
15 ml/1 tbsp chopped fresh parsley and
    croûtons, to garnish

1 Heat the oil and butter in a large flameproof casserole and fry the onions and bacon for 3–4 minutes until lightly browned. Add the mushrooms and fry for 2 minutes. Transfer to a bowl and set aside.

COOK'S TIP: *Beurre manié*, a paste for thickening casseroles, is made by blending equal amounts of butter and flour together.

2 Coat the chicken joints in seasoned flour. Add to the hot oil and butter and cook for about 5–6 minutes until browned on all sides.

3 Pour in the brandy and carefully light it with a match, then shake the pan gently until the flames subside. Pour on the wine, add the bouquet garni, garlic, sugar, salt and freshly ground black pepper.

4 Bring to the boil, cover and simmer for 1 hour, stirring occasionally. Return the reserved onions, bacon and mushrooms to the casserole, cover and cook for a further 30 minutes.

**5** Lift out the chicken, vegetables and bacon with a draining spoon and arrange on a warmed serving dish.

**6** Discard the bouquet garni, increase the heat and boil the liquid remaining in the casserole rapidly for 2 minutes to reduce it slightly.

**7** Whisk in teaspoonfuls of the prepared *beurre manié* until the liquid has thickened slightly. Pour this sauce over the cooked chicken and serve garnished with the chopped fresh parsley and croûtons.

# Spicy Clay-pot Chicken

Clay-pot cooking stems from the practice of burying a glazed pot in the embers of an open fire. The gentle heat surrounds the base and keeps the liquid inside at a slow simmer, similar to the modern-day casserole.

Serves 4–6

INGREDIENTS
1.5 kg/3–3½ lb chicken
45 ml/3 tbsp freshly grated coconut
30 ml/2 tbsp oil
2 shallots or 1 small onion,
　finely chopped
2 garlic cloves, crushed
5 cm/2 in piece lemon grass
2.5 cm/1 in piece galangal or fresh root
　ginger, peeled and thinly sliced
2 small green chillies, seeded and
　finely chopped
1 cm/½ in cube shrimp paste or
　15 ml/1 tbsp fish sauce
400 ml/14 fl oz/1⅔ cups can
　coconut milk
300 ml/½ pint/1¼ cups
　chicken stock
2 kaffir lime leaves (optional)
15 ml/1 tbsp sugar
15 ml/1 tbsp rice or white
　wine vinegar
2 ripe tomatoes and 30 ml/2 tbsp chopped
　fresh coriander, to garnish
boiled rice, to serve

**1** Preheat the oven to 180°C/350°F/ Gas 4. Joint the chicken, remove the skin from the individual pieces, together with as many of the bones as possible. This will make the final dish easier to eat.

**2** Dry fry the coconut in a large wok or heavy-based frying pan until brown. Add the oil, shallots or onion, garlic, lemon grass, galangal or ginger, chilli and shrimp paste or fish sauce. Fry briefly to release the flavours. Add the chicken and brown for 2–3 minutes.

**3** Strain the coconut milk and add the thin part with the chicken stock, lime leaves, if using, sugar and vinegar. Transfer to a glazed clay pot, cover and bake for 50–55 minutes or until chicken is tender. Stir in the thick part of the coconut milk and return to the oven for 5–10 minutes to thicken.

**4** Place the tomatoes in a bowl and cover with boiling water to loosen and remove the skins. Halve the tomatoes, discarding the seeds, and cut into large dice. Add the tomatoes to the finished dish, scatter with chopped coriander and serve with a bowl of rice.

# Apricot & Chicken Casserole

A mild and fruity curried chicken dish served with almond rice.

Serves 4

INGREDIENTS
15 ml/1 tbsp oil
8 large boned and skinned chicken thighs,
    cut into 4 pieces
1 medium onion, finely chopped
5 ml/1 tsp medium curry powder
30 ml/2 tbsp plain flour
450 ml/¾ pint/scant 2 cups
    chicken stock
juice of 1 large orange
8 dried apricots, halved
15 ml/1 tbsp sultanas
salt and freshly ground
    black pepper

FOR THE ALMOND RICE
225 g/8 oz/2 cups cooked rice
15 g/½ oz/1 tbsp butter
50 g/2 oz/½ cup toasted almonds

**1** Preheat the oven to 190°C/375°F/ Gas 5. Heat the oil in a large frying pan. Cut the chicken into cubes and brown quickly all over in the oil. Add the chopped onion and cook gently until soft and lightly browned.

COOK'S TIP: To reheat the rice, place in a pan with the butter over a very gentle heat. It may help to add a little water.

**2** Transfer to a large flameproof casserole, sprinkle in the curry powder and cook again for a few minutes. Add the flour and blend in the chicken stock and orange juice. Bring to the boil and season with salt and freshly ground black pepper.

**3** Add the halved apricots and sultanas, then cover with a lid and transfer to the oven. Cook the casserole gently for 1 hour or until the chicken pieces are tender. Adjust the seasoning according to taste.

**4** To make the almond rice, reheat the pre-cooked rice with the butter and season to taste with salt and freshly ground black pepper.

**5** Just before serving, stir the toasted almonds into the rice and serve with the chicken casserole.

# Turkey with Madeira

This casserole is served with flambéed apples and patty pan squashes.

Serves 4

INGREDIENTS
675 g/1½ lb turkey breast fillets, cut into
   2 cm/¾ in slices
65 g/2½ oz/5 tbsp butter
4 tart apples, peeled and sliced
90 ml/6 tbsp Madeira
150 ml/¼ pint/⅔ cup chicken stock
3 bay leaves, plus extra, to garnish
10 ml/2 tsp cornflour
150 ml/¼ pint/⅔ cup double cream
salt and freshly ground black pepper

**1** Preheat the oven to 180°C/350°F/
Gas 4. Season the turkey and fry in
50 g/2 oz/4 tbsp of the butter to seal.
Transfer to a casserole. Fry two of the
sliced apples gently for 1–2 minutes
and add to the turkey.

**2** Add 60 ml/4 tbsp of the Madeira,
the chicken stock and bay leaves and
allow to simmer for a couple of
minutes. Cover and cook in the oven
for about 40 minutes.

**3** Blend the cornflour with a little of
the double cream, then add the rest
of the cream. Add this mixture to the
casserole, put back in the oven and
cook for 10 minutes more to thicken
the sauce.

**4** Gently fry the remaining apple
slices in the rest of the butter. Add the
remaining Madeira and set alight.
Once the flames have died down,
continue to fry the apples until lightly
browned. Serve the casserole garnished
with the apples, squashes and bay leaves.

# Duck & Chestnut Casserole

Serve this with a mixture of mashed potatoes and celeriac, to soak up the rich duck juices.

Serves 4–6

INGREDIENTS
1.75 kg/4–4½ lb duck
45 ml/3 tbsp olive oil
175 g/6 oz small onions
50 g/2 oz field mushrooms
50 g/2 oz shiitake mushrooms
300 ml/½ pint/1¼ cups red wine
300 ml/½ pint/1¼ cups beef stock
225 g/8 oz canned, peeled,
    unsweetened chestnuts, drained
salt and freshly ground
    black pepper
fresh flat leaf parsley, to garnish
mashed potatoes and celeriac,
    to serve

1 Preheat the oven to 180°C/350°F/ Gas 4. Joint the duck into eight pieces. Heat the oil in a frying pan and brown the duck. Remove from the pan.

2 Add the onions to the pan and brown for 10 minutes. Add the mushrooms and cook for a few minutes more. Deglaze the pan with the wine and boil to reduce by half.

3 Transfer the wine and vegetables to a casserole and add the stock. Replace the duck, add the chestnuts, season, and cook in the oven for 1½ hours. Garnish with parsley and serve with mashed potatoes and celeriac.

# Pheasant with Juniper & Port

A warming winter casserole, flavoured with juniper and thyme, that brings together the rich tastes of game and port.

Serves 4

INGREDIENTS
2 pheasants
8 rindless smoked bacon rashers
30 ml/2 tbsp sunflower oil
2 celery sticks, sliced
12 pickling onions
3 carrots, sliced
8 bay leaves
8 fresh thyme sprigs
2.5 ml/½ tsp juniper berries
60 ml/4 tbsp port
600 ml/1 pint/2½ cups game stock
15 ml/1 tbsp cornflour, mixed to a paste
    with water
30 ml/2 tbsp redcurrant jelly
salt and freshly ground black pepper

**1** Preheat the oven to 190°C/375°F/ Gas 5. Cut each pheasant into four pieces. Wrap each in a rasher of bacon and tie with strong thread. This helps to keep the pheasant moist.

**2** Heat the oil in a shallow flameproof casserole and fry the pheasant portions until browned. Lift out with tongs on to a plate. Add the celery, onions and carrots to the casserole, with more oil if needed, and cook for 5–7 minutes until golden, stirring occasionally.

**3** Push a bay leaf and a sprig of thyme under the thread on each pheasant portion and arrange them on top of the vegetables.

**4** Add the juniper berries to the casserole, pour in the port and stock and season the pheasant portions to taste with salt and pepper.

**5** Cover the casserole and place in the oven. Cook for 1 hour, then stir in the cornflour paste and redcurrant jelly. Cook for about 15 minutes more or until the pheasant is tender and the sauce has thickened slightly. Serve.

# Steak with Stout & Potatoes

Meat and vegetables are cooked together in this robust stew, which needs only a green salad to make a perfect main course.

Serves 4

INGREDIENTS

675 g/1½ lb stewing or braising steak
15 ml/1 tbsp oil
25 g/1 oz/2 tbsp butter
225 g/8 oz baby or pickling onions
175 ml/6 fl oz/¾ cup stout
300 ml/½ pint/1¼ cups beef stock
1 bouquet garni
675 g/1½ lb potatoes, cut into
   thick slices
225 g/8 oz field mushrooms,
   sliced if large
15 g/½ oz/2 tbsp plain flour
2.5 ml/½ tsp mild mustard
salt and freshly ground
   black pepper
fresh thyme sprigs,
   to garnish

**1** Trim any excess fat from the steak and cut into four pieces. Season both sides of the meat. Heat the oil and half the butter in a large, heavy pan. Brown both sides of the meat, taking care not to burn the butter. Remove from the pan and set aside.

COOK'S TIP: To peel small onions, put them in a bowl and cover with boiling water. Leave to soak for about 5 minutes, then drain. The skins should peel away easily.

**2** Add the onions to the pan and brown, over a medium heat, for 3–4 minutes. Return the steak to the pan. Pour over the stout and beef stock and season to taste with salt and freshly ground black pepper.

**3** Add the bouquet garni and the potato slices to the pan. Cover the pan with a tight-fitting lid and leave to simmer over a gentle heat for 1 hour.

**4** Add the mushrooms. Replace the lid and cook for a further 30 minutes. Remove the meat and vegetables with a slotted spoon and arrange on a serving platter.

**5** Mix the remaining butter with the flour to make a *beurre manié*. Whisk a little at a time into the cooking liquid. Stir in the mustard. Cook for 2–3 minutes until thickened. Season and pour over the meat. Garnish with thyme sprigs and serve.

# Boeuf Bourguignon

Tradition dictates that you should use the same wine in this stew that you plan to serve with it, but a less expensive, full-bodied wine will do for cooking if you prefer.

Serves 6

INGREDIENTS
175 g/6 oz lean salt pork, diced, or thick-cut
    rindless streaky bacon, cut crossways
    into thin strips
1.5 kg/3–3½ lb lean stewing steak
    (chuck or shin), cut into
    5 cm/2 in pieces
40 g/1½ oz/3 tbsp butter
350 g/12 oz baby onions
350 g/12 oz small button mushrooms
1 onion, finely chopped
1 carrot, finely chopped
2 or 3 garlic cloves, finely chopped
45 ml/3 tbsp plain flour
750 ml/1¼ pints/3 cups red wine,
    preferably Burgundy
25 ml/1½ tbsp tomato purée
1 bouquet garni
600–750 ml/1–1¼ pints/2½–3 cups
    beef stock
15 ml/1 tbsp chopped fresh parsley
salt and freshly ground black pepper

**1** In a large, heavy flameproof casserole, cook the pork or bacon until it is golden brown, then remove and drain. Pour off all but 30 ml/2 tbsp of the fat.

**2** Brown the steak in batches (do not crowd the pan or the meat will not brown), then set aside on a plate.

**3** In a heavy frying pan, melt one-third of the butter and cook the baby onions until evenly golden. Set aside on a plate. In the same pan, melt half of the remaining butter and sauté the button mushrooms until they are golden, then remove from the pan and set aside with the baby onions.

**4** Pour off any fat from the casserole in which the beef was browned, add the remaining butter and fry the chopped onion, carrot and garlic for 3–4 minutes until just softened. Sprinkle the flour over the vegetables and cook for 2 minutes.

**5** Add the wine, tomato purée and bouquet garni. Bring to the boil. Return the beef and bacon to the casserole and add the stock and seasoning. Cover and simmer very gently for 3 hours or until the meat is very tender.

**6** Add the sautéed button mushrooms and baby onions to the casserole and continue to cook, covered, for a further 30 minutes. Discard the bouquet garni and stir in the chopped fresh parsley before serving.

# Braised Beef in a Rich Peanut Sauce

Flavours of the East blend together to make this a memorable dish. Rice and peanuts are used to thicken the juices, making a rich, glossy sauce.

Serves 4–6

INGREDIENTS
30 ml/2 tbsp oil
15 ml/1 tbsp annatto seeds or 5 ml/1 tsp
    paprika and a pinch of turmeric
2 medium onions, chopped
2 garlic cloves, crushed
275 g/10 oz celeriac or swede, peeled and
    roughly chopped
900 g/2 lb stewing steak, chuck, shin or
    blade, cut into 5 cm/2 in cubes
450 ml/¾ pint/scant 2 cups beef stock
350 g/12 oz new potatoes, peeled and cut
    into large dice
15 ml/1 tbsp fish or anchovy sauce
30 ml/2 tbsp tamarind sauce
10 ml/2 tsp sugar
1 bay leaf
1 fresh thyme sprig
50 g/2 oz peanuts or 30 ml/2 tbsp
    peanut butter
45 ml/3 tbsp long grain rice, soaked in water
15 ml/1 tbsp white wine vinegar
salt and freshly ground black pepper

**1** Heat the oil in a flameproof casserole, add the annatto seeds, if using, and stir to colour the oil dark red. Remove the seeds with a slotted spoon and discard. If you are not using annatto seeds, paprika and turmeric can be added later.

**2** Soften the onions, garlic and celeriac or swede in the oil without letting them colour. If you are not using annatto seeds, stir the paprika and turmeric in with the beef. Add the stock, potatoes, fish or anchovy and tamarind sauces, sugar, bay leaf and thyme. Simmer for 2 hours.

**3** Roast the peanuts, if using, under a hot grill, then rub off the skins with a clean cloth. Drain the rice and grind with the roasted peanuts or the peanut butter, using a pestle and mortar or a food processor.

**4** When the beef is tender, transfer 60 ml/4 tbsp of the cooking liquid to the ground rice and nut mixture. Blend smoothly and stir into the casserole. Simmer gently for 15–20 minutes to thicken. Stir in the white wine vinegar, season well with salt and freshly ground black pepper and serve.

# Beef Stew with Cep Dumplings

As if the temptation of a rich beef stew were not enough, here it is crowned with cep dumplings.

Serves 4

INGREDIENTS
60 ml/4 tbsp oil
900 g/2 lb chuck steak, diced
150 ml/¼ pint/⅔ cup red wine
2 medium onions, halved and sliced
½ celery stick, chopped
450 g/1 lb open-cap wild or cultivated
    mushrooms, sliced
½ garlic clove, crushed
600 ml/1 pint/2½ cups beef stock
30 ml/2 tbsp tomato purée
10 ml/2 tsp black olive purée
15 ml/1 tbsp wine vinegar
5 ml/1 tsp anchovy sauce
1 fresh thyme sprig
salt and freshly ground
    black pepper

FOR THE CEP DUMPLINGS
275 g/10 oz/2½ cups
    self-raising flour
2.5 ml/½ tsp salt
115 g/4 oz/½ cup cold butter,
    finely diced
45 ml/3 tbsp chopped fresh parsley
5 ml/1 tsp chopped fresh thyme
dried ceps, soaked in warm water
    for 20 minutes
250 ml/8 fl oz/1 cup
    cold milk

1 Preheat the oven to 160°C/325°F/ Gas 3. Heat half of the oil in a pan and brown the meat in batches. Transfer to a flameproof casserole and pour off the fat from the pan. Add the wine to the pan and stir to loosen the sediment. Pour over the meat.

2 Wipe the pan clean, then heat the remaining oil, add the sliced onions and chopped celery and brown lightly. Add to the casserole with the remaining ingredients. Bring the mixture to a simmer, cover and cook in the oven for 1½–2 hours.

3 To make the dumplings, sift the flour and salt together, add the butter, then the parsley and thyme. Drain the ceps and chop finely. Add the ceps and milk to the mixture and stir with a knife to make a soft dough, taking care not to overmix.

**4** Flour your hands and form the mixture into thumb-sized dumplings. Drop them into simmering water and cook, uncovered, for 10–12 minutes. When cooked, remove and arrange on top of the stew before serving.

VARIATION: You might like to try making the cep dumplings with other ingredients. Try watercress in place of the parsley and thyme, or add a little grated Parmesan cheese.

# Veal Stew with Tomatoes

The combination of tomatoes and orange in this dish brings to mind Mediterranean sunshine.

Serves 6

INGREDIENTS
60 ml/4 tbsp plain flour
1.5 kg/3 lb boneless veal shoulder,
    cut into 4 cm/1½ in pieces
30–45 ml/2–3 tbsp olive oil
4 or 5 shallots, finely chopped
2 garlic cloves, very finely chopped
300 ml/½ pint/1¼ cups dry white wine
450 g/1 lb tomatoes, peeled, seeded
    and chopped
grated rind and juice of 1 unwaxed orange
1 bouquet garni
15 ml/1 tbsp tomato purée
15 g/½ oz/1 tbsp butter
350 g/12 oz button mushrooms,
    quartered if large
salt and freshly ground black pepper
chopped fresh parsley, to garnish
creamy mashed potatoes, to serve

**2** Heat 30 ml/2 tbsp of the oil in a flameproof casserole and brown the meat in batches, adding more oil as necessary (do not overcrowd the pan or the meat will not brown). Set aside on a plate.

**3** In the same pan, cook the shallots and garlic until just softened, then stir in the dry white wine and bring the mixture to the boil. Return the meat to the pan and add the chopped tomatoes, orange rind and juice, bouquet garni and tomato purée. Bring back to the boil, cover and simmer gently for 1 hour.

**1** Put the flour and seasoning in a plastic bag, drop in the pieces of meat a few at a time and shake to coat, tapping off the excess.

**4** Melt the butter in a frying pan and sauté the mushrooms until golden. Add the mushrooms to the casserole and cook, covered, for 20–30 minutes, or until the meat is very tender. Adjust the seasoning and discard the bouquet garni. Garnish with parsley and serve with mashed potatoes.

COOK'S TIP: Veal shoulder is generally sold boned and rolled into a joint. One particular shoulder joint is called an oyster joint, and is a little leaner than ordinary shoulder. Knuckle is another cut of veal often used for stewing.

# Lamb Tagine

Combining meat, dried fruit and spices is typical of Middle-eastern cooking. This type of casserole takes its name from the earthenware pot (tagine) in which it is traditionally cooked.

Serves 4–6

INGREDIENTS
115 g/4 oz/½ cup dried apricots
30 ml/2 tbsp olive oil
1 large onion, chopped
1 kg/2¼ lb boneless shoulder of lamb, cubed
5 ml/1 tsp ground cumin
5 ml/1 tsp ground coriander
5 ml/1 tsp ground cinnamon
grated rind and juice of ½ orange
5 ml/1 tsp saffron strands
15 ml/1 tbsp ground almonds
about 300 ml/½ pint/1¼ cups lamb or
    chicken stock
15 ml/1 tbsp sesame seeds
salt and freshly ground black pepper
fresh parsley, to garnish
couscous, to serve

**1** Cut the apricots in half and put in a bowl with 150 ml/¼ pint/⅔ cup water. Leave to soak overnight.

**2** Preheat the oven to 180°C/350°F/Gas 4. Heat the oil in a flameproof casserole, add the onion and cook gently for 10 minutes until it is soft and golden.

**3** Stir in the lamb. Add the cumin, coriander and cinnamon, and season. Stir to coat the lamb in the spices. Cook, stirring, for 5 minutes.

**4** Add the apricots and their soaking liquid. Stir in the orange rind and juice, saffron, ground almonds and enough stock to cover. Cover the casserole and cook in the oven for 1–1½ hours until the meat is tender, stirring occasionally and adding extra stock if necessary.

**5** Heat a heavy-based frying pan, add the sesame seeds and dry fry them, shaking the pan, until they are golden. Sprinkle the sesame seeds over the meat, garnish with fresh parsley and serve with couscous.

# Irish Stew

Simple and delicious, this is the quintessential Irish main course.

Serves 4

INGREDIENTS
1.5 kg/3 lb boneless lamb chops
15 ml/1 tbsp oil
3 large onions, quartered
4 large carrots, thickly sliced
900 ml/1½ pints/3¾ cups water
4 large potatoes, cut into chunks
1 large fresh thyme sprig
15 g/½ oz/1 tbsp butter
15 ml/1 tbsp chopped fresh parsley
salt and freshly ground black pepper
Savoy cabbage, to serve (optional)

**1** Trim any fat from the lamb. Heat the oil in a flameproof casserole and brown the meat on both sides. Remove from the pan.

**2** Add the onions and carrots to the casserole and cook for 5 minutes until the onions are browned.

**3** Return the meat to the pan with the water. Bring to the boil, cover and simmer for 1 hour. Add the potatoes and thyme and cook for a further 1 hour.

**4** Leave the stew to settle for a few minutes. Remove the fat from the top of the liquid with a ladle, then pour off the liquid into a clean saucepan.

**5** Stir in the butter and parsley. Season well and pour back into the casserole. Serve with Savoy cabbage, if liked.

# Slow-cooked Lamb with Barley

A meltingly tender result is achieved by using an electric slow-cooker.

Serves 4–6

INGREDIENTS
15–30 ml/1–2 tbsp oil
900 g/2 lb shoulder of lamb, cubed
2 large onions
6 carrots or potatoes
115 g/4 oz/⅔ cup barley
750 ml–1.2 litres/1¼–2 pints/3–5 cups
   boiling stock
salt and freshly ground black pepper
chopped fresh thyme,
   to garnish

1 Heat half the oil in a frying pan and sauté the lamb in batches until brown. Transfer to a plate.

2 Cut the onions and carrots into small pieces (thinly slice the potatoes, if using) and sauté in the remaining oil. Add the barley and seasoning, pour in half the stock and bring to the boil. Cook for about 5 minutes.

3 Pour the vegetables and barley into the base of a slow-cooker, cover with the lamb cubes and add enough stock to make a gravy. Cover and cook for 6–9 hours. Alternatively, cook, tightly covered, in a conventional oven preheated to 110°C/225°F/ Gas ¼, adding more stock as needed. Adjust the seasoning, stir well and serve garnished with thyme.

# Spanish Black Bean Stew

This simple stew, reminiscent of a French cassoulet, uses a few robust ingredients to create a deliciously intense flavour.

Serves 5–6

### INGREDIENTS
275 g/10 oz/1½ cups black beans
60 ml/4 tbsp olive oil
350 g/12 oz baby onions
2 celery sticks, thickly sliced
675 g/1½ lb boneless belly pork rashers, rinded and cut into large chunks
10 ml/2 tsp paprika
150 g/5 oz chorizo sausage, cut into chunks
600 ml/1 pint/2½ cups light chicken or vegetable stock
2 green peppers, seeded and cut into large pieces
salt and freshly ground black pepper

**1** Put the beans in a bowl, cover with plenty of cold water and leave to soak overnight. Drain, put into a saucepan and cover with fresh water. Bring the water to the boil and boil rapidly for 10 minutes. Drain.

**2** Preheat the oven to 160°C/325°F/Gas 3. Heat the oil in a large frying pan and fry the onions and celery for 3 minutes. Add the pork and fry for 5–10 minutes until browned.

VARIATION: This is the sort of stew to which you can add a variety of winter vegetables such as leek, turnip, celeriac and even small potatoes.

**3** Add the paprika and chorizo sausage to the pan and fry for a further 2 minutes. Transfer the mixture to an ovenproof dish with the black beans and mix together.

**4** Add the chicken or vegetable stock to the pan and bring to the boil. Season lightly with salt and freshly ground black pepper, then pour over the meat and beans. Cover and bake for 1 hour.

**5** Stir the green peppers into the stew and return to the oven for a further 15 minutes. Serve hot.

# Fruity Cider Pork with Parsley Dumplings

Pork and fruit are a perfect combination. If you don't want to make dumplings, serve creamy mashed potatoes with the stew.

Serves 6

INGREDIENTS

115 g/4 oz/scant ½ cup pitted prunes,
    roughly chopped
115 g/4 oz/½ cup dried apricots,
    roughly chopped
300 ml/½ pint/1¼ cups dry cider
675 g/1½ lb lean boneless
    pork, cubed
30 ml/2 tbsp plain flour
30 ml/2 tbsp oil
350 g/12 oz onions,
    roughly chopped
2 garlic cloves, crushed
6 celery sticks, roughly chopped
475 ml/16 fl oz/2 cups stock
12 juniper berries,
    lightly crushed
30 ml/2 tbsp chopped fresh thyme
425 g/15 oz can black-eyed
    beans, drained

FOR THE DUMPLINGS
115 g/4 oz self-raising flour
50 g/2 oz/generous ⅓ cup shredded
    vegetable suet
45 ml/3 tbsp chopped fresh parsley
salt and freshly ground
    black pepper

**1** Preheat the oven to 180°C/350°F/ Gas 4. Soak the prunes and apricots in the cider for at least 20 minutes.

**2** Toss the pork in seasoned plain flour to coat; reserve any leftover flour. Heat the oil in a large flameproof casserole and brown the meat in batches. Drain on kitchen paper.

**3** Add the onions, garlic and celery to the casserole and cook for 5 minutes. Add any remaining plain flour and cook for a further 1 minute.

**4** Add the stock, the cider and fruit, juniper berries, thyme and seasoning. Bring to the boil, add the pork, cover and cook in the oven for 50 minutes.

**5** To make the dumplings, sift the flour into a bowl, then stir in the suet and parsley. Add about 90 ml/6 tbsp water and mix to form a dough.

**6** Stir the beans into the casserole and adjust the seasoning. Divide the dumpling mixture into six, form into rounds and place on top.

**7** Return the stew to the oven and cook, covered, for a further 20–25 minutes or until the dumplings are cooked and the pork is tender. Serve.

# Smoked Bacon, Sausage & Bean Stew

Simple and inexpensive to make, this will quickly become a favourite family supper.

Serves 6

INGREDIENTS
150 g/5 oz/¾ cup each dried black-eyed, pinto and cannellini beans, soaked overnight in cold water
15 ml/1 tbsp olive oil
6 rindless smoked streaky bacon rashers
6 large pork sausages
3 large carrots, halved
3 large onions, halved
1 small garlic bulb, separated into cloves
4 bay leaves
2 fresh thyme sprigs, plus extra to garnish
15–30 ml/1–2 tbsp dried green peppercorns
300 ml/½ pint/1¼ cups unsalted vegetable stock or water
300 ml/½ pint/1¼ cups red wine
salt and freshly ground black pepper
green salad, to serve

**1** Bring a large saucepan of unsalted water to the boil. Add the drained beans and boil vigorously for 30 minutes. Drain and set aside.

**2** Pour the olive oil into a large, heavy-based flameproof casserole, then lay the streaky bacon rashers on top. Add the pork sausages, together with the halved carrots and onions.

**3** Peel, but do not slice the garlic cloves, then press them into the mixture with the bay leaves, thyme sprigs and the dried peppercorns. Spoon the cooked, drained beans over the top of the mixture.

**4** Pour in the stock or water and wine. Cover and bring to the boil. Reduce the heat to the lowest setting and cook for 4–6 hours, stirring periodically and topping up the liquid if necessary.

**5** Stir the mixture and season to taste with salt and freshly ground black pepper. Serve garnished with thyme and accompanied by a green salad.

# Harvest Vegetable & Lentil Casserole

A warming and nutritious combination of brown or green lentils and seven different vegetables.

Serves 6

INGREDIENTS
15 ml/1 tbsp sunflower oil
2 leeks, sliced
1 garlic clove, crushed
4 celery sticks, chopped
2 carrots, sliced
2 parsnips, diced
1 sweet potato, diced
225 g/8 oz swede, diced
175 g/6 oz/⅔ cup whole brown or
   green lentils
450 g/1 lb tomatoes, peeled,
   seeded and chopped
15 ml/1 tbsp chopped fresh thyme
15 ml/1 tbsp chopped fresh marjoram
900 ml/1½ pints/3¾ cups well-flavoured
   vegetable stock
15 ml/1 tbsp cornflour
salt and freshly ground
   black pepper
fresh thyme sprigs,
   to garnish

**1** Preheat the oven to 180°C/350°F/ Gas 4. Heat the oil in a large flameproof casserole.

**2** Add the leeks, garlic and the chopped celery to the casserole and cook the vegetables over a low heat for 3 minutes, stirring occasionally.

**3** Add the carrots, parsnips, sweet potato, swede, lentils, tomatoes, chopped herbs, stock and seasoning. Stir well. Bring to the boil, stirring the mixture occasionally.

**4** Cover and bake in the oven for about 50 minutes until the vegetables and lentils are cooked and tender, stirring once or twice during the cooking time.

**5** Blend the cornflour with 45 ml/ 3 tbsp water in a small bowl. Stir it into the casserole and heat gently on top of the stove, stirring continuously, until the mixture comes to the boil and thickens, then simmer gently for 2 minutes, stirring.

**6** Spoon the casserole on to warmed serving plates or into bowls and serve garnished with thyme sprigs.

# Chick-pea Stew

This hearty chick-pea and vegetable stew makes a filling meal. It is delicious served with garlic-flavoured mashed potatoes.

Serves 4

INGREDIENTS
30 ml/2 tbsp olive oil
1 small onion, chopped
225 g/8 oz carrots, halved and
    thinly sliced
2.5 ml/½ tsp ground cumin
5 ml/1 tsp ground coriander
30 ml/2 tbsp plain flour
225 g/8 oz courgettes, sliced
200 g/7 oz can sweetcorn, drained
400 g/14 oz can chick-peas, drained
30 ml/2 tbsp tomato purée
200 ml/7 fl oz/scant 1 cup hot
    vegetable stock
salt and freshly ground
    black pepper
garlic-flavoured mashed potatoes,
    to serve (optional)

**2** Add the ground cumin, coriander and flour. Stir and cook for 1 minute. Cut the courgette slices in half and add them to the pan.

**3** Add the sweetcorn, chick-peas, tomato purée and hot vegetable stock. Stir well. Bring the mixture to the boil, then simmer gently for 10 minutes, stirring frequently.

**1** Heat the oil in a frying pan. Add the onion and carrots. Toss to coat the vegetables in the oil, then cook over a moderate heat for 4 minutes.

COOK'S TIP: For speedy garlic-flavoured mashed potatoes, simply mash boiled potatoes with garlic butter and stir in chopped fresh parsley and a little crème fraîche.

**4** Taste the stew and add salt and freshly ground black pepper according to taste. Serve the stew immediately, accompanied by garlic-flavoured mashed potatoes (see Cook's Tip), if liked.

# Winter Casserole with Herb Dumplings

When the cold weather draws in, gather together a good selection of vegetables and make this comforting casserole with some hearty, old-fashioned dumplings.

Serves 6

### INGREDIENTS

2 potatoes
2 carrots
1 small fennel bulb
1 small swede
2 leeks
2 courgettes
50 g/2 oz/4 tbsp butter or margarine
30 ml/2 tbsp plain flour
425 g/15 oz can butter beans, with liquor
600 ml/1 pint/2½ cups vegetable stock
30 ml/2 tbsp tomato purée
1 cinnamon stick
10 ml/2 tsp ground coriander
2.5 ml/½ tsp ground ginger
2 bay leaves
salt and freshly ground black pepper

### FOR THE DUMPLINGS

200 g/7 oz/scant 2 cups plain flour
115 g/4 oz shredded vegetable suet, or
   chilled butter, grated
5 ml/1 tsp dried thyme
5 ml/1 tsp salt
120 ml/4 fl oz/½ cup milk

**1** Cut all the vegetables into even, bite-size chunks and fry them gently in the butter or margarine for about 10 minutes.

**2** Stir in the flour, the liquor from the beans, the stock, tomato purée, cinnamon stick, ground coriander, ground ginger, bay leaves and seasoning. Bring to the boil, stirring. Cover and simmer for 10 minutes, then add the beans and cook for a further 5 minutes.

**3** To make the herb dumplings, simply mix the flour, shredded vegetable suet or chilled butter, dried thyme and salt to a firm but moist dough with the milk. Knead with your hands until the dough is smooth.

**4** Divide the dough into 12 pieces, rolling each one into a ball with your fingers. Place them on top of the simmering stew, allowing space between each one for expansion. Continue to simmer gently, with the lid on, for a further 15 minutes.

**5** Remove the cinnamon stick and bay leaves before you serve the dish, steaming hot.

COOK'S TIP: Do not lift the lid during the final stage, and do not cook the dumplings too fast.

59

# Kenyan Mung Bean Casserole

This lightly spiced dish is an unusual way of preparing mung beans.

Serves 4

### INGREDIENTS
225 g/8 oz/1¼ cups mung beans,
    soaked overnight in cold water
25 g/1 oz/2 tbsp
    ghee or butter
2 garlic cloves, crushed
1 red onion, chopped
30 ml/2 tbsp tomato purée
½ green pepper, seeded and cut into
    small cubes
½ red pepper, seeded and cut into
    small cubes
1 green chilli, seeded and
    finely chopped
300 ml/½ pint/1¼ cups water

**2** Heat the ghee or butter in a separate saucepan, add the crushed garlic and chopped onion and fry for 4–5 minutes until golden brown, then add the tomato purée and cook for a further 2–3 minutes, stirring all the time.

**1** Put the mung beans in a large saucepan, cover with water and boil until the beans are soft and the water has evaporated. Remove from the heat and mash roughly with a fork or potato masher.

**3** Stir in the mashed beans, then the green and red peppers and chilli.

COOK'S TIP: If you prefer a more traditional texture, cook the mung beans until very soft, then mash them thoroughly until smooth.

**4** Add the measured water to the casserole, stirring well to mix all the ingredients together.

**5** Pour the casserole into a clean saucepan and allow to simmer for about 10 minutes, stirring occasionally. Spoon into a serving dish and serve at once.

# Vegetarian Cassoulet

Every town in south-west France has its own recipe for this popular classic. Here is a hearty vegetable version.

Serves 4–6

## INGREDIENTS
400 g/14 oz/2 cups dried haricot beans,
   soaked overnight in plenty of cold water
1 bay leaf
2 onions
3 cloves
2 garlic cloves, crushed
5 ml/1 tsp olive oil
2 leeks, thickly sliced
12 baby carrots
115 g/4 oz button mushrooms
400 g/14 oz can chopped tomatoes
15 ml/1 tbsp tomato purée
5 ml/1 tsp paprika
15 ml/1 tbsp chopped fresh thyme
30 ml/2 tbsp chopped fresh parsley
115 g/4 oz/2 cups fresh
   white breadcrumbs
salt and freshly ground black pepper

**1** Drain the beans and rinse under cold running water. Put them in a saucepan together with 1.75 litres/ 3 pints/7½ cups cold water and the bay leaf. Bring to the boil and cook rapidly for 10 minutes.

**2** Spike one of the onions with cloves. Add to the beans and reduce the heat. Cover and simmer gently for 1 hour until the beans are almost tender. Drain, reserving the stock but discarding the bay leaf and onion.

**3** Chop the remaining onion and put it into a large flameproof casserole together with the crushed garlic cloves and the olive oil. Cook gently for 5 minutes, or until softened, stirring occasionally to prevent sticking.

**4** Preheat the oven to 160°C/325°F/ Gas 3. Add the sliced leeks, baby carrots, button mushrooms, chopped tomatoes, tomato purée, paprika and chopped fresh thyme to the casserole, followed by 400 ml/14 fl oz/1⅔ cups of the reserved bean stock. Bring the mixture to the boil, cover and allow to simmer for 10 minutes.

COOK'S TIP: If you're short of time use canned haricot beans – you'll need two 400 g/14 oz cans. Drain, reserving the bean juices, and make up to 400 ml/14 fl oz/ 1⅔ cups with vegetable stock.

**5** Stir in the cooked beans and the parsley. Season to taste with salt and freshly ground black pepper. Sprinkle the breadcrumbs on top and bake, uncovered, in the oven for 35 minutes or until the topping is golden brown and crisp. Serve.

# Index

First published in 1999 by Lorenz Books © Anness Publishing Limited 1999

Lorenz Books is an imprint of Anness Publishing Limited, Hermes House, 88–89 Blackfriars Road, London SE1 8HA

This edition distributed in Canada by Raincoast Books, 8680 Cambie Street, Vancouver, British Columbia, V6P 6M9

ISBN 0 7548 0321 X

A CIP catalogue record for this book is available from the British Library.

Publisher: Joanna Lorenz
Editor: Valerie Ferguson
Series Designer: Bobbie Colgate Stone
Designer: Andrew Heath
Production Controller: Joanna King

Recipes contributed by: Catherine Atkinson, Carole Clements, Roz Denny, Michelle Derriedale-Johnson, Patrizia Diemling, Matthew Drennan, Sarah Edmonds, Joanna Farrow, Sarah Gates, Rosamund Grant, Deh-Ta Hsiung, Judy Jackson, Lesley Mackley, Sue Maggs, Norma Miller, Katherine Richmond, Anne Sheasby, Liz Trigg, Steven Wheeler, Elizabeth Wolf-Cohen

Photography: Edward Allwright, Steve Baxter, James Duncan, John Freeman, Michelle Garrett, Amanda Heywood, David Jordan, Patrick McLeavey, Michael Michaels, Thomas Odulate

1 3 5 7 9 10 8 6 4 2

Notes:
For all recipes, quantities are given in both metric and imperial measures and, where appropriate, measures are also given in standard cups and spoons. Follow one set, but not a mixture, because they are not interchangeable.

Standard spoon and cup measures are level.

1 tsp = 5 ml   1 tbsp =15 ml

1 cup = 250 ml/8 fl oz

Australian standard tablespoons are 20 ml. Australian readers should use 3 tsp in place of 1 tbsp for measuring small quantities of gelatine, cornflour, salt, etc.

Medium eggs are used unless otherwise stated.

Printed and bound in Singapore